P9-DCP-871

AFRO-BETS®
FIRST BOOK ABOUT
AFRICA

AN INTRODUCTION FOR YOUNG READERS
by Veronica Freeman Ellis
illustrated by George Ford

Editorial Direction and Book Design	Color Rendering	Concept
Cheryl Willis Hudson	**Doris Tomaselli**	**Wade Hudson**

AFRO-BETS® is a registered trademark of Cheryl Willis Hudson. The AFRO-BETS® Kids were conceived and created by Wade Hudson and Cheryl Willis Hudson. Illustrations copyright 1989 by George Ford. Inquiries should be addressed to JUST US BOOKS, INC., 301 Main Street, Suite 24, Orange, NJ 07050.

Printed in Italy   First Edition   Library of Congress Catalog Card Number 89-85157
ISBN: 0-940975-03-3 (paper)   ISBN: 0-940975-12-2 (reinf. lib. edition)   10 9 8 7 6 5 4 3 2 1

JUST US BOOKS
Orange, New Jersey
1989

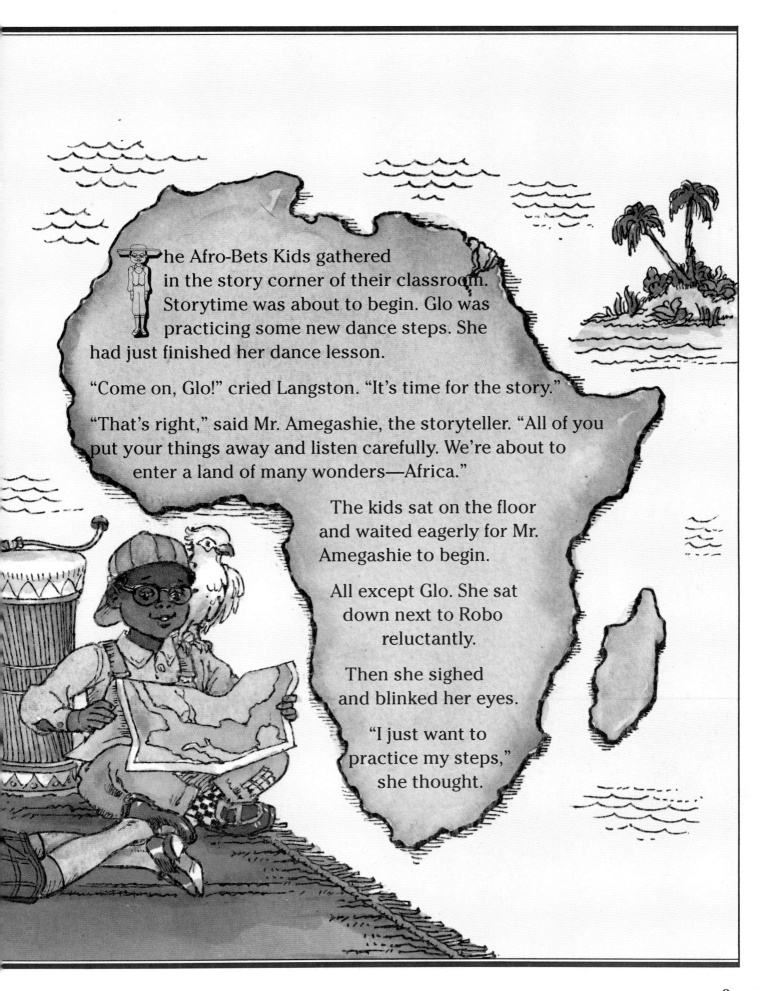

The Afro-Bets Kids gathered in the story corner of their classroom. Storytime was about to begin. Glo was practicing some new dance steps. She had just finished her dance lesson.

"Come on, Glo!" cried Langston. "It's time for the story."

"That's right," said Mr. Amegashie, the storyteller. "All of you put your things away and listen carefully. We're about to enter a land of many wonders—Africa."

The kids sat on the floor and waited eagerly for Mr. Amegashie to begin.

All except Glo. She sat down next to Robo reluctantly.

Then she sighed and blinked her eyes.

"I just want to practice my steps," she thought.

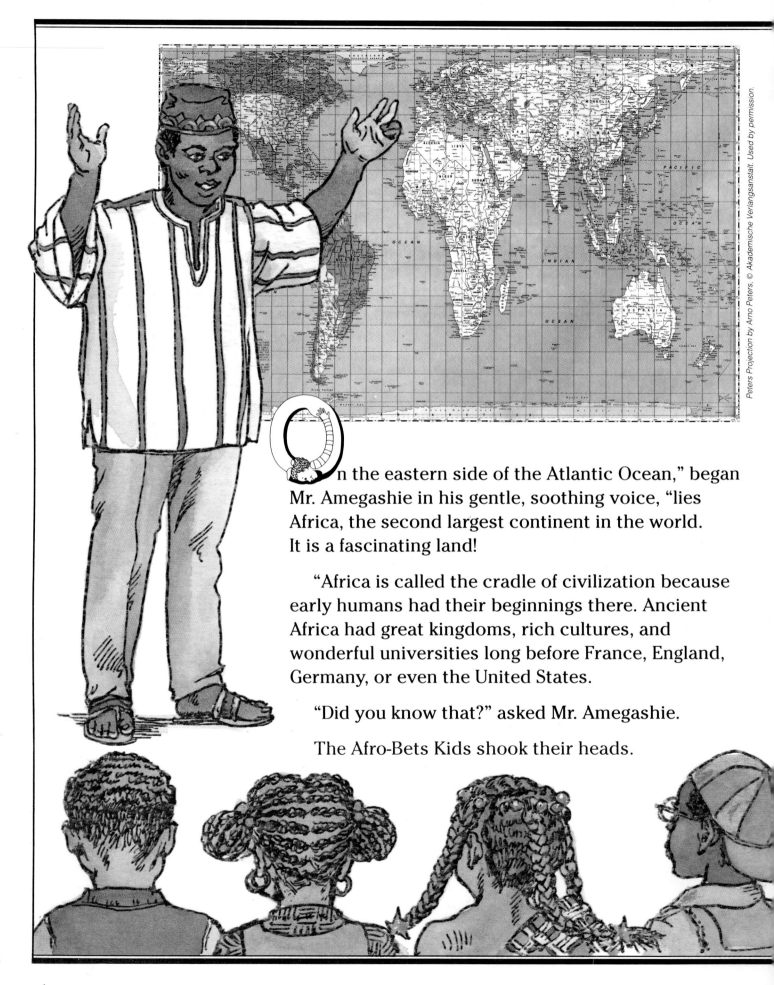

On the eastern side of the Atlantic Ocean," began Mr. Amegashie in his gentle, soothing voice, "lies Africa, the second largest continent in the world. It is a fascinating land!

"Africa is called the cradle of civilization because early humans had their beginnings there. Ancient Africa had great kingdoms, rich cultures, and wonderful universities long before France, England, Germany, or even the United States.

"Did you know that?" asked Mr. Amegashie.

The Afro-Bets Kids shook their heads.

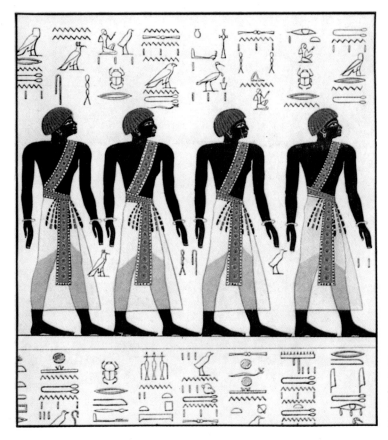

People of Kush are represented in a painting from a royal tomb located in the Valley of the Kings, Egypt. Around 1300 B.C.

"Yes, it's true," Mr. Amegashie assured them.

"You see, there were many great kingdoms—Egypt, Kush, Ethiopia…"

"I've heard about Egypt," interrupted Langston. "That's where the pyramids are."

"That's right, Langston," Mr. Amegashie said with a smile. "Egypt was one of the most powerful kingdoms. Early Egyptians were black, and they had a highly developed civilization.

"They created great works of art, wonderful structures like the pyramids, and a form of writing called hieroglyphics.

"Kush was located south of Egypt. It became a great power around 750 B.C. The Kushites conquered and ruled Egypt for about one thousand years. Kush was rich in iron ore, gold, and ivory.

"Ethiopia was an important kingdom, too. It was also called Sheba. For many years Makeda, the famous queen of Sheba, was the ruler.

"Ghana, Mali, and Songhay were famous kingdoms in West Africa during the years 500 A.D. to 1500 A.D. And were they rich! The kingdoms had so much gold that Mansa Musa, Mali's most famous ruler, gave some away on a trip he made to Mecca, the Arab holy city. In fact, he used almost one hundred camels to carry the gold and other gifts."

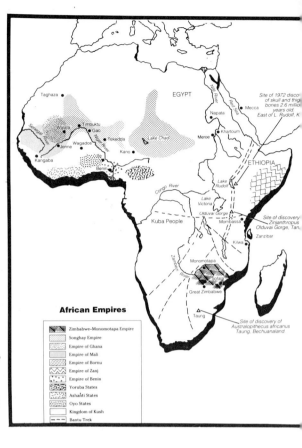

African Empires

- Zimbabwe–Monomotapa Empire
- Songhay Empire
- Empire of Ghana
- Empire of Mali
- Empire of Bornu
- Empire of Zanj
- Empire of Benin
- Yoruba States
- Ashanti States
- Oyo States
- Kingdom of Kush
- Bantu Trek

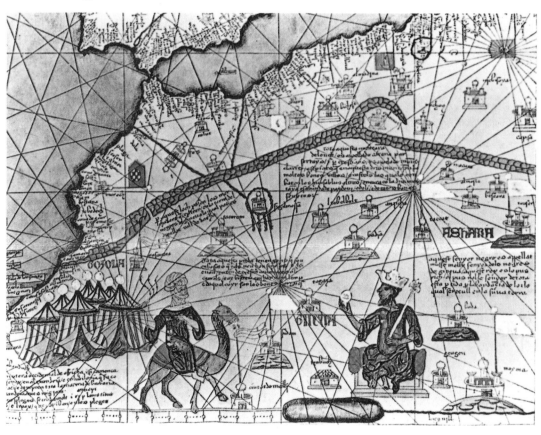

Mansa Musa of Mali barters with an Arab trader. He holds a huge gold nugget in his hand in this 1375 Catalan map.

Benin Plaque of multiple figures
Mid 16–17th century
Cast copper alloy

"Wow!" Stef exclaimed. "One hundred camels!"

"Mansa Musa established the great mosque and university of Sankore in the city of Timbuktu," continued Mr. Amegashie. "It had one of the largest libraries in the world. Another great university at Jenne, a city in Songhay, was famous for training doctors. People came from all over the Arab world to study there.

"The kingdoms were also famous for the trans-Saharan gold-salt trade. Merchants took salt into the kingdoms to trade for gold. Before entering or leaving the kingdoms, the merchants paid a tax. The taxes helped to make the kingdoms rich.

"During 1300 A.D. to 1600 A.D. Kilwa, a city-state on the East African coast, was an important trading center. Merchants there traded African gold, iron, and ivory for things from Arabia, India, and China. Ships that used Kilwa's harbor paid a tax. The taxes made Kilwa's rulers very rich."

"Were there other important kingdoms?" asked Tura.

"Kanem-Bornu was powerful during the years 800 A.D. to 1800 A.D.," said Mr. Amegashie. "It was known for its strong army.

"Benin was another powerful kingdom with a great civilization. It was located in present day southern Nigeria. Portuguese traders were so impressed by the kingdom that they asked the Oba, or king, to send one of his people to visit Portugal, as an act of friendship.

"The kingdom of the Monomotapa grew up in South-Central Africa. Its capital was at Great Zimbabwe.

Soldiers of the Kanem-Bornu army prepare to charge.

There the rulers built a Great Temple whose stone ruins are still standing."

"What happened to all the great kingdoms?" asked Robo. He looked as if he wanted to cry.

"I'm afraid they became less powerful," said Mr. Amegashie. "Wars with invading Arab armies and other African kingdoms made the empires weak. Then later came the slave trade.

"You see, in the 1400's the age of exploration began. Many Europeans sailed to West Africa for gold and other riches. They sailed to the New World, too, to make their fortunes. As farms in the New World grew into plantations, many laborers were needed to work the land."

"Is that when Africans were brought over as slaves?" asked Langston.

es," replied Mr. Amegashie. "Europeans decided Africans were just the people for that. Millions of Africans were captured by the Europeans with the help of some African chiefs and Arab traders. Tribes, encouraged by the Europeans, warred with each other—just to capture people to sell as slaves. Families were separated! Villages were destroyed!

"Africans were chained and thrown into cramped, dark spaces on slave ships. There was no room to stand and barely enough room to sit up. Africans were forced to put up with harsh treatment from the ships' crew.

Captured Africans are taken to waiting slave ships.

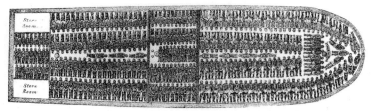

A diagram of a slave ship shows how Africans were crammed into the hull.

Rather than live as slaves, some Africans starved themselves to death. Others jumped overboard whenever they were unchained on deck. Thousands of men, women, and children died on the long journey across the Atlantic Ocean. The years of slavery were filled with cruelty and sadness. Oh, it was a horrible time in Africa's history."

The Afro-Bets Kids sat very still.

"Some of the Africans brought to America as slaves," said Mr. Amegashie, "were your ancestors. After many years of struggle, the slave trade ended, but Europeans still wanted Africa's riches. So with their guns they captured different parts of Africa, renamed them, and sent their own people to rule. Ruling someone else's country is called colonialism."

"Didn't the Africans do anything?" Tura asked.

"They fought back," said Mr. Amegashie, "and after many years they won their independence. Then the names of two famous kingdoms were reclaimed. In 1957 the Gold Coast became Ghana. In 1960 the French Sudan became Mali. Another exciting period in Africa's history had begun. It held great promises for Africa's people."

re the people in Africa all from the same tribe?" Nandi asked.

"No. No. No," answered Mr. Amegashie.

"There are many, many different people in Africa. They have different customs and speak many different languages—just like people in France, Germany, and Italy. They are all Europeans, but they have different languages and customs.

"Liberia, in West Africa, was founded by freed American slaves. Some Liberians are descendants of the freed slaves. Others are descendants of traditional Africans.

"In the cool highlands of Kenya, East Africa, live the Masai—a really tall people! They're nomads, people who go from place to place looking for food and water. They raise cattle. Masai men have long, thick hair. The women shave their heads and decorate their bodies with lots of beads and large earrings.

"The Pygmies, Africa's smallest people, live in the Central African rain forests. They are hunters and gatherers. Along the slopes of mountains in Morocco and Algeria, live the Berbers. They are farmers and cattle herders. The Tuaregs live in the Sahara Desert. The Ibo live in Nigeria. The Watutsi, who are almost seven feet tall, live in Central Africa. There are also the Zulus, who live in South Africa.

Tuareg man
Niger, West Africa

Mangbetu chief's wife
Zaire, Central Africa

"There was a time when mighty nations, such as Great Zimbabwe, flourished in southern Africa. The mightiest was the Zulu nation. The Zulus had a great king called Shaka."

"Nandi was his mother's name!" shouted Nandi.

"How wonderful to be named after her!" exclaimed Mr. Amegashie. "Shaka conquered many warring tribes and built a powerful nation. But a small group of people had come from Holland to settle in South Africa. These people are the Afrikaners. They later started apartheid, a system of oppression that forces black South Africans to live apart from Afrikaners.

"Because of apartheid, black South Africans are still not free in their own land.

"But hundreds of black South African leaders like Nelson and Winnie Mandela, Archbishop Desmond Tutu, and Oliver Tambo are working to end apartheid. When South Africa is free, all of the areas once ruled by the colonial powers will be independent nations."

Masai warrior
Kenya, East Africa

Bushman
Botswana, Southern Africa

Modern Afrikaners in period dress,
Pretoria, South Africa

"Tell us about people from your country, Mr. Amegashie," said Nandi.

"There's a wonderful story about the Ashanti people of Ghana," said the storyteller.

"Long, long time ago," he began, "the Ashanti of Ghana were many groups. Each group had its own chief. One day the chiefs were at a meeting when suddenly, a beautiful golden stool dropped from the sky. It landed gently on one chief, Osei Tutu, as he sat draped in his beautiful robe made of kente cloth. Everyone said it was a sign to become one people. Osei Tutu became the Asantehene, or king, and the Ashanti became a powerful nation. The Ashanti weave beautiful kente cloth in colorful strips. The Asantehene wears a special kente.

"Today, people of African descent live all over the world. They are as different as the many groups in Africa itself. Even though each has its own culture, all the cultures have some things that are African. In many ways, they are the same."

Chief's stool
Ashanti, Ghana
Wood, stained brown

Mr. Amegashie stopped.

"Are you kids ready for a recess?" he asked.

"No!" they answered together. All except Glo. She had a dreamy, faraway look on her face.

"I want to hear about the animals!" Stef yelled.

"Not just yet," said Mr. Amegashie. "First, let's talk about the beautiful land."

"**R**ich in natural beauty—that's Africa!" exclaimed Mr. Amegashie. "Africa is almost completely surrounded by oceans and has many beautiful beaches. The land is made up mainly of tropical rain forests, savannas, deserts, mountains, and rivers. The equator goes through Africa, and countries close to the equator have a tropical, or hot, climate.

"Tropical rain forests are hot, and they get a lot of rain. Trees there are tall with large, leafy branches.

"Savannas are wide and grassy. Some parts have bushes and small trees. In West Africa, the savanna is south of the Sahara Desert. It's also in parts of Central and East Africa.

Mbuti (pygmy) near edge of Ituri Rain Forest, Zaire

Agricultural fields along the Nile in Giza, Egypt

"The Sahara Desert—now that's a place to see! It's as large as the United States. The Sahara, the world's largest desert, wasn't always a desert.

Camel caravan passing the pyramids of Cheops and Khafre, Giza, Egypt

Thomson's gazelles roam the savanna of Serengeti, Tanzania, East Africa.

"Thousands of years before great kingdoms flourished in Africa, the Sahara was fertile and green. Over the years, rivers that flowed in the area began to dry up. Gradually the Sahara became what it is today.

Snowcapped slopes of Mt. Kilimanjaro, Kenya

"The highest mountains in Africa are Kilimanjaro and Mount Kenya. Their snowy tops are in a cold climate far away from the equator.

"The Nile is Africa's and also the world's longest river. It flows north from the Nile Valley in Egypt to the Mediterranean Sea. Other major rivers are the Congo, Niger, and Zambezi."

"Does Africa still have a lot of gold?" asked Tura.

"The African continent is rich in many natural resources. Liberia is known for its iron ore mines, and the South African diamond mines are awesome!

"Liberia is also famous for its rubber plantations. Zaire, in Central Africa, is known for both its rubber and cocoa plantations. Tea

Victoria Falls Zimbabwe, Southern Africa

Modern miners in Ashanti gold fields, Ghana

Gold pendant, Akan peoples Côte d'Ivoire Cast gold alloy ▽

is an important crop in East Africa, while coffee is important in the Ivory Coast, a West African country.

"Parts of Africa, mainly the deserts, are not good for growing crops. Droughts often take place in those areas. In the early 1980's there was a drought in the Sahel, a place between the Sahara and the West African coast. Many people died because there was no water to grow food.

"For hundreds of years Africa's deserts, rivers, and forests were barriers to travelers and traders who wanted to explore Africa's interior. As explorers gradually pushed through the barriers, they learned many fascinating things about Africa.

"Now, Stef," smiled Mr. Amegashie, "we'll talk about the animals."

U nusual and exciting animals live in Africa," said Mr. Amegashie, "and the savanna is home to many. Roaming across that wide, grassy plain in East Africa are the world's fastest land animals—cheetahs!

"Zebras, lions, and giraffes live there, too. Giraffes are the world's tallest animals. The savanna is also home to some of Africa's elephants, the world's largest land animals. Smaller elephants live in the rain forests.

"A fascinating animal called the okapi lives in the rain forests. It looks like a giraffe, an antelope, and a zebra. While monkeys chatter and swing from tree to tree in the forest, leopards silently hunt for food."

"And camels live in the desert," said Robo. "They can go without water for a long time. Right, Mr. Amegashie?"

"Right, Robo," answered Mr. Amegashie.

Chi Wara antelope headdress
Bambara, Mali
Painted wood

Equestrian figure from Inland
Delta Region, Niger River, Mali
Terra-cotta

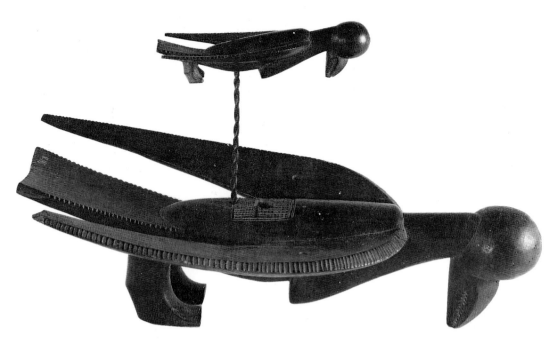

Bird staff carving of hawk and vulture
Senufo, Côte d'Ivoire
Wood, stained brown

"African birds are so colorful," continued the storyteller. "Beautiful peacocks live in the Central African rain forests. Flamingos, which are water birds, are in East and South Africa. So are ostriches, the world's biggest birds. Imagine a bird that can't fly. That's the ostrich!

"Then there are the hippos. There are two kinds in Africa. One kind weighs about eight thousand pounds. It is found all over Africa. The other is much smaller and is called a pygmy hippo. It weighs about five hundred pounds and is found only in Liberia.

"The hyena lives in West and East Africa. It's a really clever animal! If an animal dies from poison, hyenas won't eat it because they can smell the poison. Hyenas are brave, too. They'll fight any animal for food—even lions! There are many tales about the hyena."

"Can you tell us one?" asked Robo.

"Once upon a time," began Mr. Amegashie, "Hyena was a good-looking animal. His eyes sparkled, his legs were straight, and his coat glistened in the sunlight. Hyena was proud of his looks, but he was careful not to let other animals know how proud he was. Whenever an animal mentioned his good looks, Hyena replied, 'You're just being kind. I'm not good-looking at all.'

"Hyena was kind and friendly to all the animals, too. One day Leopard found an antelope that a hunter had killed. Leopard didn't know that the antelope had died from poison.

" 'Great,' thought Leopard. 'Now I don't have to hunt for food. I can eat this antelope and relax for the rest of the day.'

"Just as Leopard was about to sink his teeth into the meat Hyena appeared, as if by magic.

" 'Stop! Don't eat that antelope!' shouted Hyena.

"Now Leopard and the other animals didn't know Hyena could smell poison. Leopard was angry.

" 'Are you crazy, Hyena?' Leopard asked. 'This antelope will save me a day's work. Get out of my way and let me eat.'

" 'The antelope died from poison, Leopard,' said Hyena. 'If you eat it, you'll die, too.'

" 'I don't believe a word you say,' said Leopard. 'You want the antelope, so you've made up that poison story. Well, I'm too smart to believe it.'

"Leopard began to eat the antelope. He hadn't finished his meal when the poison began to work on him. In a little while he was dead.

"Just then Leopard's wife appeared. She saw Leopard lying dead next to the half-eaten antelope, and she saw Hyena standing nearby.

" 'You killed my husband!' shouted Mrs. Leopard. 'You'll suffer for this!'

"Hyena didn't try to explain what had happened. He knew Mrs. Leopard would never believe him. He ran off to hide, but before he could the other animals captured him. Mrs. Leopard had spread the word that Hyena had killed her husband to get the antelope.

"The animals fought Hyena. They tried to kill him but Hyena managed to escape. During the fight they destroyed his beautiful coat and broke his hind legs. That is why today hyenas have mangy, ugly coats and weak hind legs. And that's why they'll fight any animal for food."

**M**r. Amegashie stopped for a moment, but the Afro-Bets Kids did not stir. They were spellbound.

Then Mr. Amegashie picked up a little box from the table beside him and stroked it gently. The box was a kalimba, an African thumb piano.

Tura thought the sound was beautiful.

"In African society," said Mr. Amegashie, "art and music are always part of the rhythm of life. People in Africa use instruments made from all kinds of materials to make music. And everyday things are works of art. Africans decorate their musical instruments.

***Carved wood chair
Bajokwe, Southern Zaire***

"They also decorate things that they use for meals. Many village homes are painted in colorful patterns. Doors often have beautiful carvings, and combs have wonderful designs.

"Beautiful terra-cotta sculptures have been discovered in the ancient lands of Nok and Ife. Terra-cotta is a kind of clay.

"Bronze figures from Ife and the kingdom of Benin show rich examples of court life. Royal artists there made fantastic bronze plaques for the walls of the king's palace.

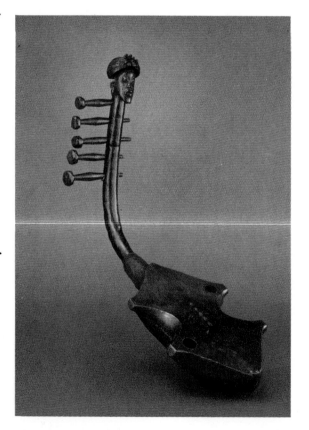

***Harp from Zande peoples of Zaire
Wood, animal hide and metal***

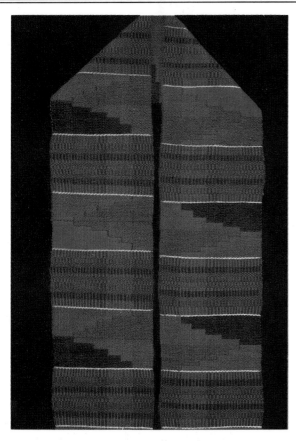

Royal commemorative head made of
cast copper alloy
Edo peoples,
Benin Kingdom
Nigeria

Kente cloth strip made of
woven silk and cotton, Ghana

"African art is exciting. Many people all over the world collect it because of its beauty and its power. In traditional religions, Africans pray to forces in the natural world. They pray to spirits in trees, rivers, and other wildlife. Many masks are created to capture spirits and forces in nature, and Africans believe the masks are sacred. Many churches in Africa are like those in the United States and Europe. Missionaries took Christianity to Africa. And many Africans are Moslems because the Arabs took Islam there. Even though many Africans practice Christianity and Islam, they also pray to their ancestors for strength, advice, and wisdom."

Tura said, "Africa's art, music, and religions are like everything African—different, rich, exciting, and powerful."

African sculpture, music, and dance all work together in celebrating the traditional African way of life," continued Mr. Amegashie. "Men, women, and children dance to celebrate many special things that happen.

Masks are worn during harvest celebrations and rites of passage. They are also used during dances for the birth of new babies, weddings, or funerals.

"Yes. Dancing is important in everyday life. Although many kinds of musical instruments are used, the drum is the most powerful, and people dance mostly to drumbeats."

Suddenly, Glo sat up straight. Her face got brighter. Mr. Amegashie was beating a drum.

"Dance? Did someone say dance?" asked Glo.

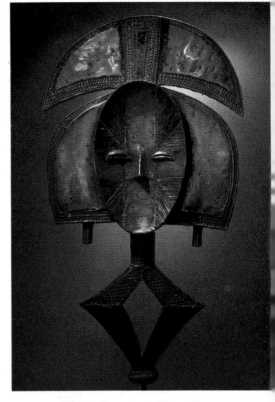

Ancestor guardian figure (Mbulu ngulu) kota, Gabon Wood, brass and copper

"I've heard of African talking drums," Stef interrupted. "Do the drums really talk?"

"Not in the way people talk," answered Mr. Amegashie. "Africans beat drums in a special way. Sometimes the sounds are messages. Slaves in the New World beat drums to send messages to one another."

Now Glo was standing up. She could hear the beat and feel the rhythm.

"Many of the dances that people do in the United States and other countries had their beginnings in Africa," continued Mr. Amegashie as he put down his drum. "Africans who were kept as slaves in the New World played songs from their homelands. The sounds of spirituals, gospel music, jazz, and rhythm and blues all come from African roots. The same is true for music in the West Indies and in South America."

"Really?" Glo asked. "I didn't know that!"

Ghanaian drummers perform at a national celebration, Accra Sports Stadium, Ghana.

African roots are deep in many parts of the world," continued the storyteller. "No matter where they go, Africans take their rich culture with them. And they bring new ways back to Africa.

"But no matter what new ways people take to Africa, family life and kinship groups remain important. These groups are the strength of African society. In many homes grandparents, parents, and children live together. And in traditional villages a household often has aunts, uncles, and cousins as well. They share one another's joys and sorrows."

"That sounds like our annual family reunion," giggled Nandi. "There's always lots of good food and music and storytelling and lots of dancing."

Female figure with a child
Baluba, Eastern Zaire
Wood

Male dancers from Mali wear Dogon
masks of wood and raffia during a
traditional harvest celebration.

Heads of state meet during a session of the Organization of African Unity, Addis Ababa, Ethiopia ▽

A reading class involving mother, son, teacher and monitor in Zaria, Northern Nigeria

Masai women return from selling crafts in main Nairobi market, Kenya.

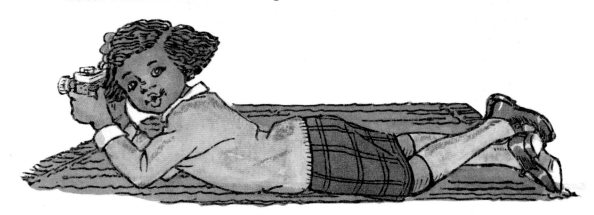

Well, that's our story about Africa," said Mr. Amegashie as he looked out at the faces of the Afro-Bets Kids. "I'd love to come and visit with you again—that is, if you'd like me to."

"Yeah!" shouted the Afro-Bets Kids together. Even Glo clapped her hands.

"Come on, Glo!" shouted Langston as they all started to leave. "Storytime's over. You were daydreaming, as usual. You missed most of it."

"You think so!" Glo exclaimed. Then she smiled mysteriously and did a few dance steps—a hop to the right, a hop to the left, a jump, and a turn. "You'd be surprised what I heard, Langston. Africa is a land of such wonder and power!"

To the Reader

Africa is a vast continent consisting of fifty-three countries and over one thousand distinct languages. Many of the names, people, and places mentioned in *Afro-Bets First Book About Africa* may be unfamiliar to you. The guide below will help you to pronounce the unfamiliar words. Accented syllables appear in boldface.

Afrikaner: ah free **kah** ner

Amegashie: ah may **gah** she

ancestor (**an** ses tor): a relative who lived hundreds of years ago

apartheid: ah **par** thide

asantehene: ah **sahn** tay **hay** nee

Ashanti: ah **shahn** tee

Benin: ben **neen**

civilization: (**siv** ver ler **zay** shun): the advanced life of a people—includes their art, writing, religion, government, and schools

colonialism: koh **low** nee ahl **lis** sem

Egypt: ee jipt

Ethiopia: ee thee **oh** pee ya

Ghana: gah nah

hieroglyphics: hy ro **gli** fix

hyena: hy ee nah

Ibo: ee bow

Ife: ee fay

Jenne: jen **nay**

kalimba: kah **leem** bah

Kanem-Bornu: kah nem bor **noo**

kente: ken tay

Kilimanjaro: kil lee mahn **jah** row

Kilwa: kil wah

Kush: koosh

Mali: mah lee

Makeda: mah kee **dah**

Mansa Musa: mahn sah moo sah

Masai: mah **sigh**

Monomotapa: mon noh moh tah pah

Osei Tutu: o **say too** too

Pygmy: pig mee

rites of passage: ceremonies that mark young people's passage into adulthood

Sankore: sahn koh **ray**

savanna: suh **van** nah

Shaka: shah kah

Songhay: sohn gay

terra-cotta: ter ruh **cot** tuh

Tuareg: twa reg

Watutsi: wah **toot** see

Zaire: zah **eer**

Zimbabwe: zeem **bahb** way

Acknowledgments
Photo credits are listed consecutively by the photographer's name and source, left to right, top to bottom in order of the appearance of each photograph. Abbreviations: NMAA/EE/SI: National Museum of African Art, Eliot Elisofon Archives, Smithsonian Institute; T: Top B: Bottom L: Left R: Right M: Middle C: Center
title page: Eliot Elisofon, NMAA/EE/SI **p. 4** World Map-Peters Projection by Arno Peters, ©Akademische Verlagsanstalt. Distributed in the U.S. by Friendship Press, used by persmission; **p. 5** detail reprinted from facsimile of plate 136, K.R. Lepsius, Denkmaeler aus Aegypten und Aethiopien, nach den zechnungender von seiher majestat Ill (Berlin, 1849–59) **p. 6** photo courtesy The British Museum; **p. 7** Jeffrey Ploskonka, NMAA/EE/SI; **p. 10L** private collection; **p. 10R** private collection; **p. 13T** Eliot Elisofon, NMAA/EE/SI; **p. 13M** Eliot Elisofon, NMAA/EE/SI; **p. 13BL** Eliot Elisofon, NMAA/EE/SI; **p. 13BC** Michael L. Yoffee, NMAA/EE/SI; **p. 13BR** © Jason Lauré, Impact Visuals; **p. 15T** Collection of the Newark Museum; **pp. 16T, 16B, 17T, 17B:** Eliot Elisofon, NMAA/EE/SI; **p. 18T** Eliot Elisofon, NMAA/EE/SI; **p. 18B** courtesy Zimbabwe Ministry of Information; **p. 19T** courtesy Africa Report; **p. 19B** Jeffrey Ploskonka, NMAA/EE/SI; **p. 20L** Collection of The Newark Museum, photo by Motter; **p. 20R** Jeffrey Ploskonka, NMAA/EE/SI; **p. 21T** Collection of The Newark Museum, photo by Armen May; **p. 24T** Courtesy, Buffalo Museum of Science; **p. 24B** Jeffrey Ploskonka, NMAA/EE/SI; **p. 25L** private collection; **p. 25R** Jeffrey Ploskonka, NMAA/EE/SI; **p. 26** from Collection of Dr. Robert Nooter and Ms. Nancy Nooter, courtesy of NMAA/EE/SI, photo by Delmar Lipp; **p. 27** Margaret A. Novicki/Africa Report; **p. 28T** Courtesy, Buffalo Museum of Science; **p. 28B** © Jason Lauré/Impact Visuals; **p. 29L** UNICEF photo by E. & M. Bernheim; **p. 29L** Betty Press/Africa Report; **p. 29B** Betty Press/Africa Report.

The publisher acknowledges with special thanks the following persons who generously contributed their time and talents during the production of this book: Anita Jenkins and Judith Luskey, NMAA/EE/SI; Alana Lee, Africa Report; Wendy Lewison, Doris Tomaselli, Margaret Trejo, Wade Hudson, Vera C. Mitchell, and B. G. Short.

Veronica Freeman Ellis, a native of Liberia, West Africa, has a heritage that reaches out from, and back to, Africa. Some of her ancestors were brought to the United States as slaves, and in the 1800s her maternal great grandmother emigrated from Mississippi to Liberia. A graduate of Boston University and the Northeastern University Graduate School of Education, Ms. Ellis has taught African Culture and English, and has worked for several years as a reading textbook editor. She lives in Massachusetts with her husband and two children. This is her first book for young readers.

George Ford is a distinguished artist who has illustrated more than two dozen juvenile picture books. He grew up in the Brownsville and Bedford-Stuyvesant sections of Brooklyn and spent some of his early years on the West Indian Island of Barbados. Among the books Mr. Ford has illustrated are *Muhammad Ali*, *Far Eastern Beginnings*, *Paul Robeson*, *Ego Tripping*, *Darlene* and *Ray Charles*, for which he won the American Library Association's Coretta Scott King Award. Mr. Ford lives in Brooklyn with his wife and daughter.